Who Has This Tail?

Laura Hulbert
illustrated by Erik Brooks

SCHOLASTIC INC.

Who has this tail?

A spider monkey has this tail.

A spider monkey uses its tail
to hang on to branches.

Who has this tail?

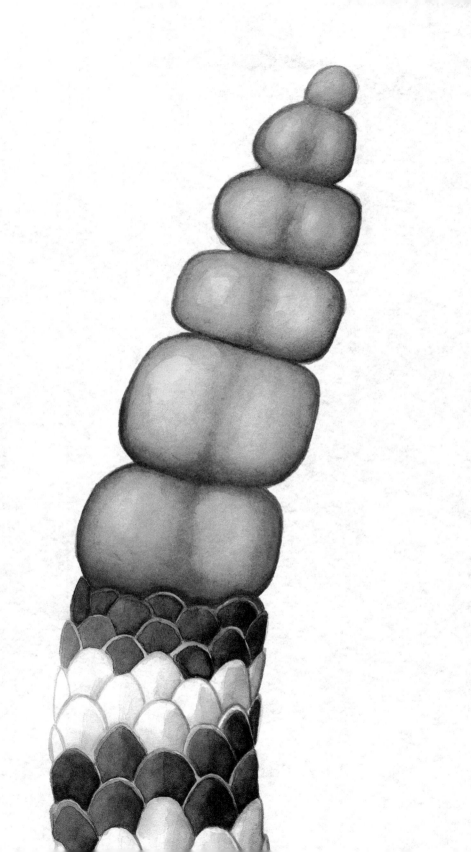

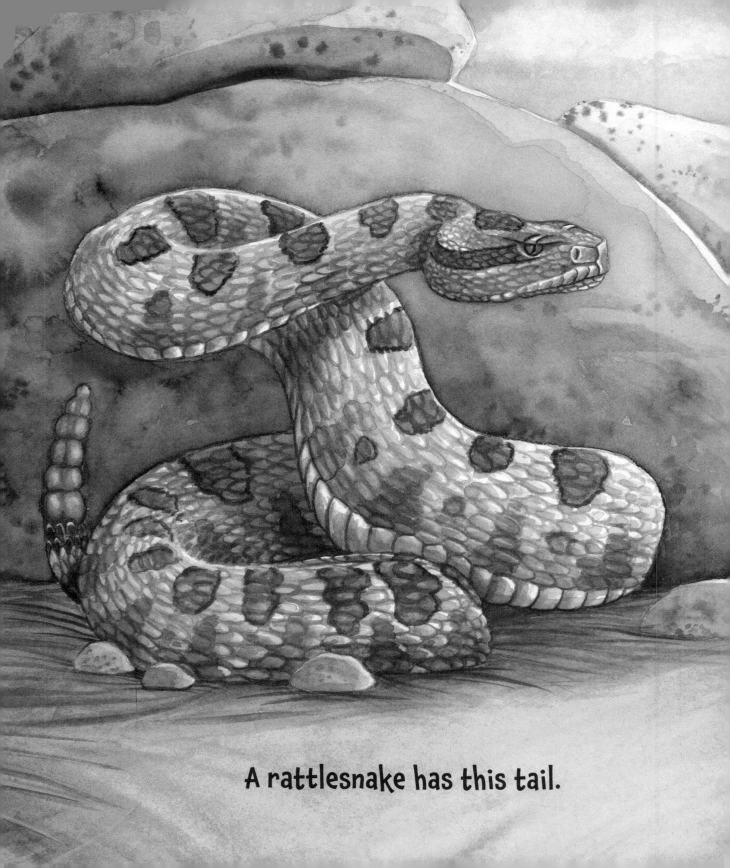

A rattlesnake has this tail.

A rattlesnake uses its tail to warn its enemies.

Who has this tail?

A shark has this tail.

A shark uses its tail to push
itself through the water.

Who has this tail?

A gerbil has this tail.

A gerbil uses its tail to balance on its back legs.

Who has this tail?

A horse has this tail.

A horse uses its tail
to flick away flies.

Who has this tail?

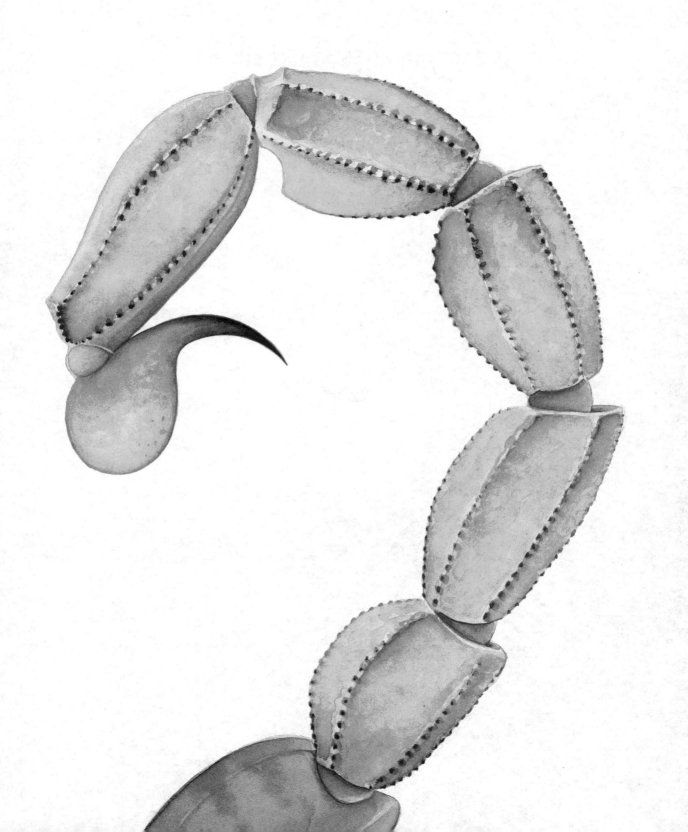

A scorpion has this tail.

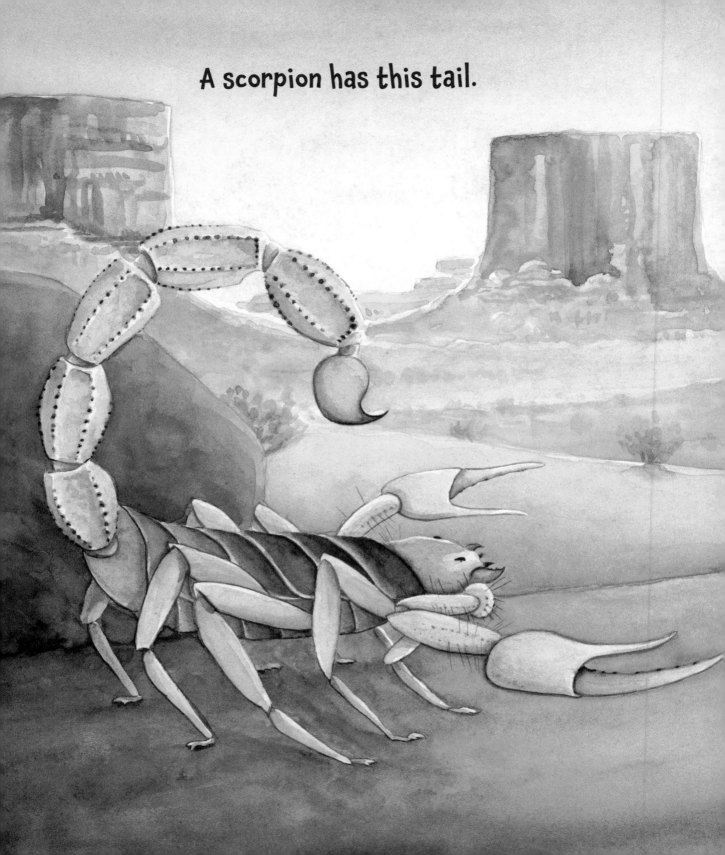

A scorpion uses its tail to sting its prey.

Who has this tail?

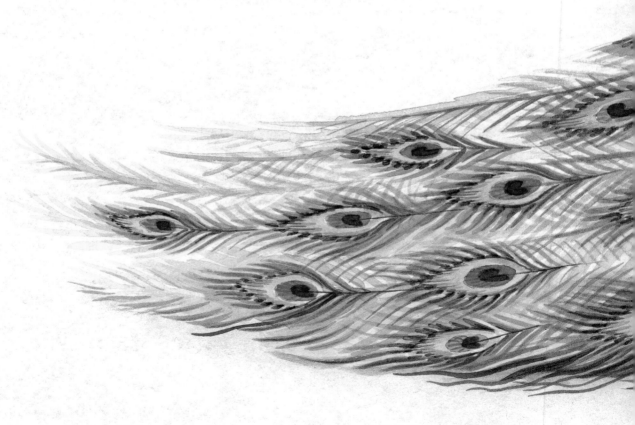

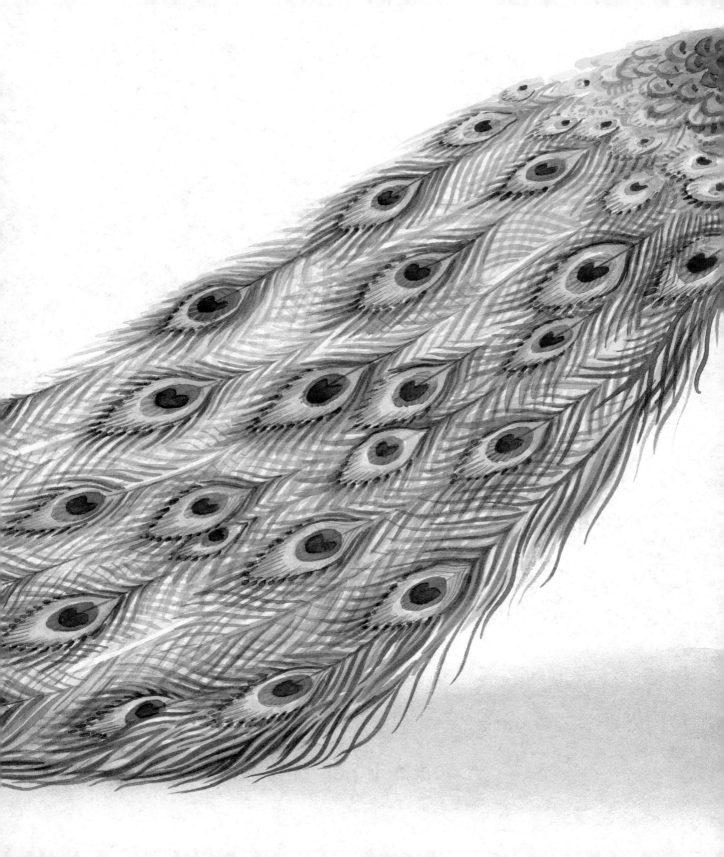

A peacock has this tail.

A peacock uses its tail
to attract a mate.

Who has this tail?

An Arctic fox has this tail.

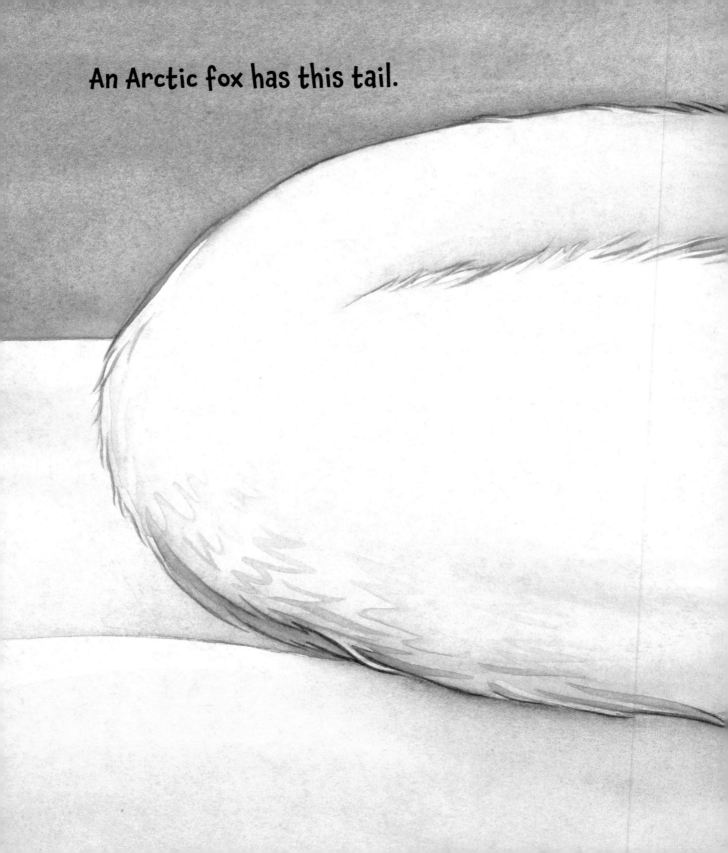

An Arctic fox uses its tail
to stay warm when it sleeps.

Who has this tail?

A beaver has this tail.

A beaver uses its tail to steer in the water.

We have

Who

has

open here →

these

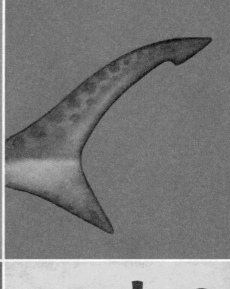

tails?

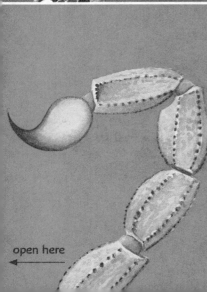

open here ←

these tails!

For Mary
—L. H.

For Will, who landed tailfirst
—E. B.

ISBN 978-0-545-66157-7

16 15 14 13 12 11 10 9 8 7 6 5   15 16 17 18 19 20/0

Printed in the U.S.A.   08

First Scholastic printing, November 2013

The artist used watercolor on paper to create the illustrations for this book.